Armenian Church, James Issaverdens

The Armenian Ritual

Volume 2

Armenian Church, James Issaverdens

The Armenian Ritual
Volume 2

ISBN/EAN: 9783337288440

Printed in Europe, USA, Canada, Australia, Japan

Cover: Foto ©Andreas Hilbeck / pixelio.de

More available books at **www.hansebooks.com**

THE ARMENIAN RITUAL

PART II.

THE DIVINE ORDINANCES

ACCORDING TO

THE ARMENIAN RITUAL

Being a translation from the original
in the Armenian language; to which is added
a few explanatory paragraphs

BY

F. JAMES Dr. ISSAVERDENZ

Second edition

VENICE

PRINTED IN THE ARMENIAN MONASTERY OF St. LAZARO

1873

TO Mr. F. COLTON,

CONSUL OF THE UNITED STATES OF AMERICA

AT VENICE

It was in September of last year, that I had the honour to receive you, when for the first time you came to visit this Armenian Institution at San Lazzaro, in the Lagune of Venice. The day was one of great beauty, and you well remember it, as adding so much to the pleasure of your visit; while I shall ever remember the occasion as being the commencement of your sincere and valued friendship. You were accompanied by some acquaintances who, as well as yourself, were much interested in all questions relating to the administration of the Sacraments in the Armenian Church. This led me to write something on the subject, as also to add literal translations from the Original Armenian; and now when the work is finished I send it forth, hoping that it may be agreeable to you, and useful to others.

Believe me to be always your faithful friend

F. JAMES Dr. ISSAVERDENZ

Armenian Monastery of San Lazzaro

June. 30. 1867.

CONCERNING THE ARMENIAN RITUAL.

The first essential and regular arrangement of the Armenian Ritual, as we find mentioned in the Armenian national history, was made towards the beginning of the fifth century; at which time there lived the most celebrated doctors of the Armenian Church, St. Isaac and St. Mesrob-the first, translator of the Bible into Armenian, the latter, inventor of the Armenian Alphabet-and both fitted to adorn the Armenian Church with wise rules and disciplines, and enrich the Armenian Ritual with such ceremonies as they thought proper to introduce from other systems of the east, in conformity with the national spirit.

By such a wise arrangement, principally, the Armenians came to possess a ritual of the Church, that, properly may be said, to be one of their highest national glories, and which after the surname of its principal compiler is called *Mashdotz* (Մաշտոց).

In the course of succeeding times this Ritual was enriched, by other celebrated Armenian doctors, with such prayers and benedictions, as they thought proper to introduce from foreign Rituals.

Of this Ritual there are to be found about fifty manuscript copies in the Armenian library in Venice, the oldest of which is a large one, in folio size, written on parchment, and, as it seems probable, in the beginning of the eighth century.

It was in 1832 after a scrupulous comparison of all these manuscripts, the first edition of the Armenian Ritual was published in Venice, by the Mekitaristican society of San Lazzaro.

And now making use of that first edition, I translate, word for word, the prayers of the Sacrament of Baptism and Confirmation, as well as those of the ceremony which is to be performed by the mother of the Child.

To these I have an idea to join some notices of the administration of other Sacraments, which I think would not be without interest to those who wish to know something in regard to the eastern rites.

I.

A FEW NOTICES CONCERNING THE ADMINISTRATION OF THE SACRAMENT OF BAPTISM ACCORDING THE ARMENIAN RITUAL.

The first rule we find in the Armenian Ritual for the administration of the Sacrament of Baptism, is the instruction it gives in regard to adults, who, not yet christians through Baptism, aspire to become so.

These, the Ritual admonishes not to baptize and not to allow them to enter the Church, before three weeks, or more, during which time they have studied as catechumens, all the doctrines of the faith of the Church of Christ. During this time of exercise, the duty of the teacher will be always to exhort to prayer the person who aspires to baptism.

After having been made acquainted with all the truths of the faith of Christ, he may be baptized after the manner adopted for little children.

As for little children, they will be baptized on the eighth day after their birth, - except in cases where there is danger of death. - The Godfather brings the child to the Churh, where the priest and the deacons perform the ceremony after the rules of the Ritual.

II.

It is a custom in the Armenian Church to tie around the head of the newly baptized person, like a crown, a string or riband, twisted of red and white threads, at the end of which hangs a small cross. This crowning typefies the graces of the Holy Spirit, with whom every newly baptized person is filled, through the Sacraments of Baptism and Confirmation.

This kind of crown or string, is prepared or twisted, in the beginning of the ceremony of baptism, while reciting the CXXX. psalm; at which time they twist together the red and white threads. But it is tied round the head of the Child after he has received the Sacrament of Confirmation, as the reader may find in the course of the prayers of that sacrament. And this crown is to be worn continually for eight days; after which time, during a short prayer, it is taken off by the priest.

III.

The fount or the basin of baptism, is ordinarily placed in a particular chapel, the entrance to which opens into the Church. It is always cut in stone, and cannot be made of any other material. The first part of the prayers of the ceremony, are performed outside of the door of the baptistery, as is recommended by the ritual, in the words «*out of the doors of the Church*».

IV.

The duty of blessing the oil they make use of in the ceremony of baptism, belongs to the priest who performs the ceremony of the sacrament upon the catechumen, and is done during the time he is reciting the prayers, and in such quantity only as is sufficient for that one ceremony; so that nothing of it remains. This we find recommended by the Armenian patriarch, John the Philosopher, (718) in his writings: « It is the priest 's duty » he says, « to bless the oil of baptism during the ceremony, and in as great a quantity as is requisite for the occasion; and in the meantime to finish that by applying it to the person that receives the sacrament of baptism; and dare not a second or more times bless the oil that once was blessed. That is to be used only for the unction of the catechumens during the time they are baptized in the fount and dare not make any use of the same in other sacrament of unction ».

Formerly it was the custom of the Armenian Church to anoint also the catechumen outside the doors of the baptistery with this oil, and introduce him afterwards near the fount. But with time this custom was laid aside, as not an essential ceremony.

V.

The essential part of baptism is to pour water, with the hand, upon the head of the catechumen three times, pronouncing separately, each time, the name of, *Father*, *Son*, and *Holy Ghost*. After which they were wont to immerse the catechumen three times under the water; but this ceremony, is secondery, and typefies the participation in the interment of Christ, through which the original sin is buried, and through the grace of Christ the newly baptized becomes worthy to be inscribed in the number of those that are affiliated to God.

VI.

In this way is to be baptized immediately the new born child when it is in danger of death; which ceremony may be performed by any one present, though not a churchman, by pouring only water upon the head. But if it recovers from its sickness, it should to be carried into the Church, where they will perform all the ceremony, except the pouring of the water three times upon its head.

The Sacrament of Confirmation was regarded by the eastern Church from all antiquity as an essential point to be administrated early to the faithful, that they might acquire the assistance of the grace of the Holy Ghost. The dangers of life which might arise from any cause and under any circumstances through sicknesses or persecutions, persuaded her priests to apply the administration of that holy Sacrament immediately after the ceremony of baptism; so that, on all occasions, the faithful might find themselves fortified with the graces of the Holy Spirit.

It is for the same reason that the Armenians also were accustomed till now to administer that Sacrament together with that of baptism. But contrary to the custom of the western Church that Sacrament is performed by the same priest who administers the sacrament of baptism.

After he has ended the ceremony of baptism, he anoints with the holy Chrism the nine members of the body of the newly baptized, as may be seen in the course of the prayers connected with that ceremony.

Afterwich he blesses also the clothes of the child, and clothing him, he crowns his head with the string or ribbon which they have twisted in the beginning of the ceremony of baptism, which typefies the grace of the Holy Spirit, as said before.

And now if the newly baptized be an adult, he partakes of the holy Sacrament of Communion; or if a new-born child, they make him partake of that holy Sacrament, by touching his lips with the holy Body of our Lord Christ. (*)

These two ceremonies being over, if the newly baptized person be a child, they carry him home; if an adult, there is a rule to observe. He is obliged not to move from the Church for seven days, continually clothed in white dress, and having his head covered with a white linen. His duty will be to perform the service in the church, and spend his time always in prayer, partaking every day of the Holy Sacrament of Communion.

(*) In this way they make him partake of the Holy Communion; but ordinarily these ceremonies are performed during the Holy Mass: and then, after the priest has confirmed him and made him worship before the altar and the holy Cross, he brings him to the officiating priest at the time he is consuming the Holy Sacrament, who weting his forefinger in the Holy Blood, he puts it in the mouth of the child, saying: « May this be as cure to thy soul and body: Plenitude of the Holy Spirit ».

COMMENCEMENT OF THE CEREMONY FOR THE ADMINISTRATION OF THE HOLY SACRAMENT OF BAPTISM.

They begin to recite the CXXXst. psalm, dedicated to the twisting of the string for the crown.

Lord, my heart is not haughty, nor mine eyes lofty: neither do I exercise myself in great matters, or in things too high for me.

Surely I have behaved and quieted myself, as a child that is weaned of his mother: my soul is even as a weaned child.

Let Israel hope in the Lord from henceforth and for ever.

Glory be to the Father, to the Son and to the Holy Ghost; now and throughout all ages.

DEACON. — Let us again pray the Lord for peace: receive, save and have mercy upon us.

The Priest makes the sign of the cross upon the string, and says;

PRIEST. — Blessing and glory to the Father, to the Son, and to the Holy Ghost; now and throughout all ages.

Three times they repeat the psalm with the prayer in the same manner, during which time they continue to twist together the threads of the string. At the end of the third time they sing the following hymn upon the twisted string.

HYMN.

The indivisible Trinity, and his celestial power produced the light of the knowledge of God; let us glorify him with hymns.

The true Holy Ghost, who descended from heaven to-day and dwelt in the Apostles, let us glorify with hymns.

Him, whose descent to-day upon the Apostles was revealed to the prophet, in the mysteries of the redemption, let us glorify with hymns.

Deacon. — Let us pray the Lord unanimously and with faith, to grant us His merciful grace, that the almighty God may save us and have mercy upon us.

The Priest repeats three times:

God have mercy upon us.

After which he recites the following prayer upon the Catechumen:

Priest. — Lord our God, the beneficent God, who couldst not abandon mankind, deceived and estranged from Thee, excluded and fallen from the paradise of pleasures; but moved to compassion Thou didst humble Thyself from Thy high estate to our low nature; and taking all our own (nature) excepting sin, through passion and death upon the Cross, having bought our redemption and conversion, Thou didst regenerate us. Receive now also, beneficent Lord, the consecration of this Thy creature, who hastens to approach to Thy holy and only true divinity, bearing the name of christian on his person: and give to him virtue and assistance, and make him worthy of arriving at the purification of the holy fountain of Thy immaculate life, and to the inheritance of the adoption into Thy kingdom of heaven, Jesus Christ our Lord: to whom with the Father, and to Thee, Holy Ghost, belong glory, power and honour, now and throughout all ages. Amen

After this prayer, being still at the door of the Church, they begin to recite the XXVth, XXVIth, LIst, psalms, adding at the end of each of them:

Glory be to the Father, to the Son, and to the Holy Ghost, now, etc.

DEACON. — Let us pray again the Lord for peace; receive, save us, and have mercy upon us.

PRIEST. — Blessing and glory to the Father, to the Son, and to the Holy Ghost, now, etc.

Having finished with the psalms, the priest takes the Catechumen and gives him to the Godfather to hold him in his arms, saying:

PRIEST. — I was cast upon Thee from the womb: Thou art my God from my mothers belly. [1]

The Godfather kneeling receives the Catechumen in his arms, while the deacon preaches:

DEACON. — Let us pray again the Lord for peace. For this catechumen, let us pray the God who loves man, to take compassion according to his great clemency, and make him worthy by the washing of regeneration, and the robe of incorruption, to be numbered among those who believe in His

1 Psalm. XXII. 10.

name, and to save him through the grace of His clemency. Almighty Lord our God, save us and have mercy upon us.

The Priest says three times:

God have mercy upon us.

Afterwhich he recites this prayer:

PRIEST. — Receive Lord, who lovest man, this catechumen who is offered to Thee: purify his mind and his thoughts from all the deceptions of the enemy; and make him worthy to wash away, in the holy fountain, the corruption of his sins, and to be regenerated through the light of the graces of Thy Son Jesus Christ. In order that he also may glorify, together with us, the Holy Trinity, the Father, the Son and the Holy Ghost: now and throughout all ages. Amen.

DEACON. — Let us pray again the Lord for peace. For the expiation of sins, and for the pardon of faults, and in order that God's clemency may descend upon this catechumen, let us pray the Lord.

The Priest three times:

Lord have mercy upon us.

PRIEST. — Lord God great and glorified by all creatures: having put his confidence upon Thy terrible name, this Thy servant, has bowed his head to Thy holy name, to whom bends every knee both those that are in heaven, on earth, and under the earth: and every tongue should confess that Jesus Christ is Lord, to the glory of God the Father. [1] And now Lord, grant to this man participation in Thy terrible name, which has destroyed the deceptions of demons and corrupt idolatries, and overcame all satanic artifices. Look Lord with compassion upon this person: banish and remove from him, through the mention of Thy all victorious name upom him, all that is hidden by the impure demons, the thoughts, the words and the deeds and all the frauds, by which evil spirits deceive and destroy men. So that terrified by Thy victorious name they shall be cast down and tormented by invisible tortures, remove from him by oath, and let them never more return to him. Fill him with Thy celestial graces, and rejoice him with the perfect appellation of the name of Christian. And may he in due time be worthy the baptism of regeneration, and having received the Holy Ghost, may he be body and member of Thy holy Church, and living blamlessly in this world with irreproachable fidelity to christianity, may he attain to future happiness with all those who love Thy holy name; glorifying the immutable dominion of the Father, of the Son, and of the Holy Ghost; now and throughout all ages. Amen.

They recite the XCIst psalm; at the end of which:

Glory be to the Father, to the Son, etc.

DEACON. — Let us pray again the Lord for peace. For the descent of God's clemency on this catechumen, let us pray the Lord.

1 Philipp. II. 10, 11.

Priest, three times:

Lord have mercy upon us.

The Priest placing then his hand upon the Catechumen, recites the following prayer.

PRIEST. — Eternal God, we invoke Thee to come to our assistance; Thou who art the Creator of every thing, visible and invisible. This Thy servant confiding in Thy omnipotent name, comes to receive this spiritual consecration, to be made worthy of the purification of the holy fountain. And now by the grace of Thy clemency, Holy Trinity, behold we put our hands upon this Thy creature; and confirm him in the name of the Father, of the Son, and of the Holy Ghost; and interdict, through Thy name, all spirit of error, as well as the impure and dumb devil, in order that he should remove from the creature of Thy image, and from the works of Thy hands; and never more should approach to him. Listen to us our God; subdue the evil one through Thy power, and purify this Thy servant from all influence of the adversary: in order that he may, through Thy power, renounce alligiance to the enemy of our salvation.

At the end of this prayer the Priest orders the Catechumen or the Godfather to turn towards the west, and to lift up his hands in the form of renunciation; the Catechumen being with the Godfather in the left side of the Church, and the Priest in the right, the latter causes the Godfather thrice to swear as follows:

PRIEST. — We renounce thee, Satan, and all thy frauds, thy deceptions, and thy worship, thy inspirations, thy ways, thy wicked will, thy wicked angels, thy wicked ministers, thy wicked agents, and all thy wicked power.

And he askes the Catechumen or the Godfather:

PRIEST. — Dost thou renounce?

CATECHUMEN. — I do renounce.

PRIEST. — Dost thou renounce?

CATECHUMEN. — I do renounce.

PRIEST. — Dost thou truly renounce?

CATECHUMEN. — I do truly renounce.

Now the Priest orders the Catechumen to turn with the Godfather towards the east side, and gives to the Catechumen or to the Godfather to hold in the hand a lighted wax candle, and says:

PRIEST. — Turn to the light of the knowledge of God.

Now the catechumen stands with the Godfather in the right side of the church, and the Priest in the left. The Priest causes the former to make with his hands the form of requesting, and also to confess the only true divinity of the Holy Trinity, of the Father, of the Son, and of the Holy Ghost, asking them thrice, and saying as follows; viz.

PRIEST. Dost thou believe in the Holy Trinity in the Father, in the Son and in the Holy Ghost, in the three persons and in only one nature? Dost thou believe in the incarnation of Christ, in the announciation of Gabriel, in the conception, without seed, of the holy Virgin Mary, in the virginal birth of Christ, in the baptism, in the doctrine, in the betrayal, in the Cross, in the burial, in the resurrection after three days, in the divine ascension, in the sitting down at the right hand of the Father, in the future coming, in the holy catholic and apostolic Church, in the remission of sins, in the resurrection of the dead, in the judicial authority, in the recompensation according to the deedes done in each body, and in the eternal life? dost thou believe?

CATECHUMEN. I do believe.

In this way the Priest askes three times the Catechumen or the Godfather, who answers:

I do believe.

Again the Priest askes:

PRIEST. — Dost thou believe in the Father?

CATECHUMEN. — I do believe.

PRIEST. — Dost thou believe in the Son?

CATECHUMEN. — I do believe.

PRIEST. — Dost thou believe in the Holy Ghost?

CATECHUMEN. — I do believe.

Again the Priest says:

PRIEST. — Dost thou believe?

CATECHUMEN. — I do believe.

PRIEST. — Dost thou believe?

CATECHUMEN. — I do believe.

PRIEST. — Dost thou believe with faith?

CATECHUMEN. — I do believe with faith.

Now the deacon sings:

DEACON. — Hallelujah, orthi. [1]

PRIEST. — Peace † be with all.

DEACON. — And with thy spirit. Listen with fear.

PRIEST. — The holy Gospel according to St. Matthew.

[1] Ὀρθοί, *a Greek word signifying*: stand up.

Deacon. — Glory be to Thee, O Lord our God. Proschume. [1] It is God who speaks.

The Priest reads the Gospel according St. Matthew. Chapt. XXVIII. from 16 to 20.

GOSPEL

And the eleven disciples went into Galilee, unto the mountain where Jesus had appointed them.

And seeing him they adored: but some doubted.

And Jesus coming, spoke to them, saying; All power is given to me in heaven and in earth.

Going therefore, teach ye all nations; baptizing them in the name of the Father, and of the Son, and of the Holy Ghost.

Teaching them to observe all things whatsoever I have commanded you; and behold I am with you all days, even to the consummation of the world.

Deacon. — Glory be to Thee, o Lord our God.

The Priest recites the Nicean Creed:

We believe in one God, the Father Almighty, Maker of Heaven and Earth, and of all things visible and invisible; and in one Lord Jesus Christ, the only Son of God, born of the Father before all worlds. God of God, Light of Light, Very God of Very God, begotten, not made, consubstantial with the Father, by whom all things were made in Heaven and Earth, visible and invisible: who for us men and for our salvation, came down from Heaven, was incarnate by the Holy Ghost, of the Virgin Mary and

1 *A Greek word signifying*: be attentive.

was made man, and who took from her, Body, Soul and Spirit, and all that in man is, in truth and not in fiction; who suffered, was crucified and buried; who rose again the third day, and ascended with the same body into Heaven; where he sitteth at the right hand of God, and whence He shall come with the same body in the glory of the Father, to judge the quick and the dead; whose reign shall have no end. We believe also in the Holy Ghost not created, but perfect, who proceedeth from the Father and the Son, who spake in the Law, the Prophets and the holy Gospel; who descended into the Jordan, who announced the Envoy (CHRIST) and dwelt in the Saints. We believe in one Universal and Apostolic Church, in one baptism, in penance for the expiation and remission of sins, in the resurrection of the dead, in the Eternal judgment of body and soul, in the kingdom of Heaven, and in the life Eternal.

Now they take away the wax candle from the hands of the Catechumen or the Godfather and recite the CXVIIIth. psalm; at the end of which they enter into the Church (Baptistery), reciting the Cth. psalm; which ended:

Glory be to the Father, etc.

DEACON. — In the name of this holy Church let us pray God, that he may deliver us from sin, and save us by His merciful grace. All-powerful Lord, our God, save us and have mercy on us.

PRIEST. — Within the precincts of this temple, and in the presence of these sacred and divine emblems, bowing, we adore with trembling, and we glorify Thy holy, wonderful and triumphant reign, and we offer to Thee benediction and glory, together with the Father and the Holy Spirit, now and throughout endless ages. So be it.

Now they stand before the holy fountain, holding, prepared, the holy oil;

DEACON. — Let us pray again God for peace. For the descent into this oil of the graces of the all-powerful Holy Ghost. Let us pray the Lord, and say altogether with one accord.

PRIEST. — (*Three times*) Lord have mercy upon us. Be Thou, blessed Lord, our God, who hast chosen a people for priesthood and a kingdom, for a sacred nation and a special people; as in former times also Thou didst anoint, with such holiest oil, priests and kings and prophets. So now we pray Thee, beneficent Lord; send the graces of Thy Holy Spirit into this oil, in order that unto him who shall be anointed with it, it may be spiritual purification of thoughts. May he fight and subjugate by it the enemy (devil), and have the virtue to keep the precepts and perform good works, and be perfectly disciplined in the love of God. In order that with an illuminated mind he may live in this world for the salvation of his soul, and for the glory of the holy Trinity, and be worthy to attain to the inheritance of those who have loved the name of Jesus Christ our Lord; unto whom and to Thee Father, together with the Holy Ghost, belong glory, power, and honour, now and throughout all ages. Amen.

Now he pours the water, which is a little warm, in the font, by making the form of a Cross; and in the meantime they recite the XXIXth. psalm, at the end of which:

Hallelujah, hallelujah.

They read a lesson from Ezekiel. XXXVI. 25-28.

Then will I sprinkle clean water upon you, and ye shall be clean: from all your filthiness, and from all your idols, will I cleanse you.

A new heart also will I give you, and a new spirit will I put within you: and I will take away the stonheart out of your flesh, and I give you an heart of flesh.

And I will put my spirit within you, and cause you to walk in my statutes, and ye shall keep my judgments, and do them.

And ye shall dwell in the land that I gave to your fathers; and ye shall be my people, and I will be your God.

Another from St. Paul. Galatians, III. 22-29.

But the scripture hath concluded all under sin, that the promise by faith of Jesus Christ might be given to them that believe.

But before faith came, we were kept under the law, shut up unto the faith which should afterwards be revealed.

Wherefore the law was our schoolmaster to bring us unto Christ, that we might be justified by faith.

But after that faith is come, we are no longer under a schoolmaster.

For ye are all the children of God by faith in Christ Jesus.

For as many of you as have been baptized into Christ, have put on Christ.

There is neither Jew nor Greek; there is neither bond nor free; there is neither male nor female: for ye are all one in Christ Jesus.

And if ye be Christ's, then are ye Abraham's seed, and heirs according to the promise.

At the end: Hallelujah, Hallelujah, Hallelujah.

The Lord is my shepherd; I shall not want. [1]

DEACON. — Hallelujah orthi.

PRIEST. — Peace † be to all.

DEACON. — And with thy spirit. Listen with fear.

PRIEST. — The holy Gospel according to St. John.

DEACON. — Glory be to Thee, O Lord our God. Proschume. It is God who speaks.

St. John. Chapt. the IIId. from. 1-8.

GOSPEL

And there was a man of the Pharisees, named Nicodemus, a ruler of the Jews.

This man came to Jesus by night, and said to him: Rabbi, we know that thou art come a teacher from God; for no man can do these signs which thou dost, unless God be with him.

1 Psalm. XXIII. 1.

Jesus answered and said to him: Amen, amen I say to thee, unless a man be born again, he cannot see the kingdom of God.

Nicodemus saith to him: How can a man be born when he is old? can he enter a second time into his mother's womb, and be born again?

Jesus answered: Amen I say to thee, unless a man be born again of water and the Holy Ghost, he cannot enter into the kingdom of God.

That which is born of the flesh, is flesh: and that which is born of the Spirit, is spirit.

Wonder not, that I said to thee, you must be born again.

The Spirit breatheth where he will: and thou hearest his voice, but thou knowest not whence he cometh and whither he goeth; so is every one that is born of the Spirit.

DEACON. — Glory be to Thee, O Lord our God.

The Deacon preaches upon the water of baptism.

DEACON, — Let us pray again the Lord for peace.

PRIEST. — Lord have mercy upon us.

DEACON. — For the celestial peace and for the salvation of our souls, let us pray the Lord.

PRIEST. — Lord have mercy upon us.

DEACON. — For the peace of the whole world, and the stability of the holy Church, let us pray the Lord.

PRIEST. — Lord have mercy upon us.

DEACON. — For the life, and for the salvation of the soul of our Patriarch, let us pray the Lord.

PRIEST. — Lord have mercy upon us.

DEACON. — That the Lord may direct the works of the hands of this priest who baptizes, let us pray the Lord.

PRIEST. — Lord have mercy upon us.

DEACON. — For the purification of this water, that it be fitted to cooperate with the Holy Ghost, let us pray the Lord.

PRIEST. — Lord have mercy upon us.

DEACON. — In order that it may be blessed in like manner as Jordan was, through the graces of the only Son of God, who has illuminated us, let us pray the Lord.

PRIEST. — Lord have mercy upon us.

DEACON. — In order that it may become medicament to our soul and body, let us pray the Lord.

PRIEST. — Lord have mercy upon us.

DEACON. — For those regenerated ones who are baptized with this water, that they may become sons of the light and of the day, let us pray the Lord.

PRIEST. — Lord have mercy upon us.

DEACON. — Commemorating the Virgin Mary, Mother of God, S^t. John the Baptist, and S^t. Stephen, the first Martyr, and our holy Patriarch S^t. Gregory, and all the Saints; with all these let us pray the Lord.

PRIEST. — Remember them Lord, and have mercy upon us.

DEACON. — Again unitedly for our true and holy faith, let us pray the Lord.

PRIEST. — Lord have mercy upon us.

DEACON. — Let us commend ourselves, and each-other mutually, to the Lord God, all-powerful.

PRIEST. — We commend ourselves to Thee, O Lord.

DEACON. — Have mercy upon us, O Lord, according to Thy great mercy; let us say all together.

PRIEST. — Lord have mercy upon us. (*repeated thrice.*)

The Priest placing the neophyte near the Font, recites the following prayer upon the water of baptism.

PRIEST. — Thou, Lord, through Thy great power, didst create the sea and the earth, and all the creatures that are in them. Didst divide, and establish the waters in heaven, which is the residence of Thy celestial hosts, who glorify Thee incessantly. Didst send Thy holy Apostles, ordering them to preach to and baptize all the infidels, in the name of the Father, of the Son, and of the Holy Ghost. Didst decree, also, by Thy unerring word, that those who are not regenerated, through the water, should not enter into Paradise. Of which thing beeing afraid, this Thy servant, desiring Thee, who art the eternal life, came willingly to be baptized, spiritualy, with this water. We pray Thee, Lord; send Thy Holy Spirit into this water, and bless † and purify it, in the same manner that Thou didst purify Jordan by descending into it, Thou, our Lord Jesus Christ, who wast all-pure from sin, typifying thereby in this fountain of baptism, the regeneration of all men. Grant unto him through this water, by which now he is baptized, that he may obtain pardon for his sins, receive Thy Holy Spirit, be numbered with those who are affiliated with Thee heavenly Father, and be worthy of an inheritance in Thy celestial kingdom. In order that, purifyed from sin, he may live in this world according the pleasure of Thy will, and, in the future life, may receive, with all Thy saints, the infinite good blessings, and gladly glorify the Father, the Son, and the Holy Ghost, now and throughout all ages.

After this prayer the Priest pours into the water, in form of a cross, three drops of the holy oil, saying:

PRIEST. — May this water be blessed † and purifyed through the sign of the holy cross, of the holy gospel, and of the holy chrism; in the name of the Father, and of the Son, and of the holy Ghost; now and throughout all ages.

THEE PEOPLE. — So be it. Hallelujah, hallelujah, hallelujah.

Three times, the Priest and the People repeat the same thing, after which the Priest says.

PRIEST. — Glory be to the Father, to the Son, and to the Holy Ghost; now and throughout all ages.

THE PEOPLE. — Amen. So be it.

The Priest orders to unclothe the Catechumen and to make him ready for the holy purification, mean while he recites the following prayer:

PRIEST. — O Lord, who didst call this Thy servant to the purification and to the light of baptism; we pray Thee, to make him worthy of Thy eminent graces; efface from him the corruption of sin, and restore in him new life; fill him with the graces of the Holy Ghost and number him among those affiliated to Christ; to whom belongs glory, power and honour, now and throughout all ages.

He askes then the Catechumen or the Godfather:

PRIEST — What dost thou demand?

CATECHUMEN. — I demand to be baptized.

PRIEST. — Dost thou truly demand it?

CATECHUMEN. — I demand with faith to be baptized and purified from sin, to be released from the demons, and to serve God.

PRIEST. — Be it unto thee according to thy faith.

The Priest then askes the name of the Catechumen, and makes him descend into the font. If he is a child, the Priest with his left hand holds him by the neck, and with his right hand takes him by the feet, taking care to keep the head turned towards the west and the feet towards the east; the head up high, the face turned up and the feet down. Then with his right hand taking of the holy water, says as follows: viz

PRIEST. — (N. N.) servant of God, coming by his own will to the state of a catechumen, and from that state to that of baptism, is now baptized by me, in the name of the Father - *at which name with his palm he pours water upon the head of the child,* - and of the Son, - *again he pours water with the hand* - and of the Holy Ghost. - *a third time he pours water with his hand on the head of the catechumen.*

In this operation consists the essence of baptism, which the minister ought to perform with care and diligence.

Then the Priest immerses the child in the water, saying:

PRIEST. — Redeemed by the blood of Christ from the servitude of sin, receiving the liberty which arises from affiliation with Thee, heavenly Father, he becomes, coheir with Christ, and a temple of Thy Holy Spirit.

Thrice he recites these last words, and thrice immerses him under the water, burying thus the original sin; and typifying by it Christ's sepulture of three days. Washing then the whole body, he says:

PRIEST. — Ye that were baptized in Christ, have been clothed Christ, hallelujah; and ye that were illuminated in God the Father, may the Holy Ghost rejoice in ye, hallelujah.

Afterwards they recite the XXXIVth. psalm; but if the person baptized be a child, they recite only the first three verses. At the end:

DEACON, — Hallelujah, orthi.

PRIEST. — Peace † be with all.

DEACON. — And with thy spirit. Listen with fear.

PRIEST. — The holy Gospel according to S^t^. Matthew.

DEACON. — Glory be to Thee, O Lord our God. Proschume. It is God who speaks.

He reads the Gospel, St. Matthew Chapt. the IIId. 13-17.

GOSPEL

Then cometh Jesus from Galilee to the Jordan, unto John, to be baptized of him.

But John stayed him, saying: I ought to be baptized of thee, and comest thou to me?

And Jesus answering, said to him: Suffer it to be so now: for so it becometh us to fulfil all justice. Then he suffered him.

And Jesus, being baptized, forthwith came out of the water; and, lo, the heavens were opened to him; and he saw the Spirit of God descending as a dove, and coming upon him.

And behold a voice from heaven, saying: This is my beloved Son, in whom I am well pleased.

DEACON. — Glory be to Thee Lord, our God.

Saying the words: « *And Jesus, being baptized, forthwith came out of the water* », he takes out from the font the Catechumen, and gives him to the Godfather, and continues to read the last verse of the Gospel.

Then he recites the Lord' s prayer, for the Catechumen who has become a son of God. Afterwards he recites the following prayer.

PRIEST. — Thou Lord God, who didst illuminate Thy creatures, sending down the light of the knowledge of God in Thy servants, hast also released and purified this one, justified, and received him to affiliation with Thyself. Grant him grace to conform himself to Thy will in this life, and make him worthy of the eternal purification, joining him to the number of Thy beloved saints through the merits of our Lord Jesus Christ. To whom with the Father and the Holy Ghost belong glory, power, and honour; now and throughout all ages. Amen.

Peace † be to all. Let us adore God.

Thou God, who art great and eternal, and knowest all that is hidden; who art holy and dwellst among the saints, and savest all men; who grantest Thy knowledge to those who believe in Thee; and hast given to them the right to become sons of God, through the regeneration of the water and spirit: in which way thou didst renew this Thy servant (N. N.) through the expiation of the holy fountain; sanctify him through Thy Truth; fill him with the graces of Thy Holy Spirit; in order that he may become a temple and residence for Thy holy name, and may go forward in the way of justice, and present himself joyfully and without fear at the terrible tribunal of Thy only Son, our Lord Jesus Christ. To whom belong glory, power, and honour; now and throughout all ages.

After having ended the prayers of the Sacrament of Baptism, the Priest taking in his right hand the little flask which contains the holy Chrism, begins with the others to sing the Hymn belonging to the holy oil, which is as follows: viz.

HYMN

Celestial Father, who formerly in the laws of Moses didst give virtue to the oil of the Sanctuary, for anointing those who were destined to be anointed, as an example of Thy only Son; pour Thou also into this oil Thy celestial graces.

Oh Christ, anointed of God! Thy name was called «oil poured» - *according to Solomon*, - and as Thou didst descend among us, and uniting Thy divinity to our nature, Thou didst anoint it, so also into this oil too, pour Thy celestial graces.

Thou Holy Ghost, who didst descend in the holy room among the Apostles, as anointer of the anointed men, and in anointing them didst, through them, regenerate us, terrestial creatures, and hast made us sons of God; pour Thou also into this oil, Thy celestial graces.

Oh Thou, who through this oil dost adorn Thy

holy bride the Church with spiritual vestments of graces and gifts; her sons together with the angels praise Thee, O Holy Trinity.

After this Hymn the Priest with his right thumb takes of the holy Chrism, and confirms with it the nine members of the Catechumen's body.

First, the forehead, saying:

PRIEST. — This sweet oil † is poured upon thee in the name of Christ, as a seal of the celestial gifts.

Second, the eyes, saying:

PRIEST. — May this seal † which is offered to thee in the name of Jesus Christ, illuminate thine eyes, lest thou sleep the sleep of death. [1]

Third, the ears, saying:

PRIEST. — May this anointment of sanctification † make thee obedient to the commandments of God.

Fourth, the nose, saying:

PRIEST. — May this seal † which is given to thee in the name of Jesus Christ, be to thee as a sweet savour of life unto life. [2]

Fifth, the mouth, saying:

PRIEST. — May This seal † which is given to thee in the name of Jesus Christ, be to thee as a watch, and as a solid door to thy lips. [3]

Sixth, both the palms, saying:

PRIEST. — May this seal † which is given to thee in the name of Jesus Christ, cause thee to be beneficent, and virtuous, and to do good works.

1 Psalm. XIIIth. 3.
2 II. Corinth. II. 15. 16.
3 Psalm. CXLIst. 3.

Seventh, the heart, saying:

PRIEST. — May this seal of divine cleansing † create in thee a clean heart, and renew a right spirit within thee. [1]

Eighth, the spine, saying.

PRIEST. — May this seal † which is given to thee in the name of Jesus Christ, be to thee a powerful shield; wherewith thou mayest be able to quench all the fiery darts of the wicked. [2]

Ninth, the feet, saying:

PRIEST. — May this divine seal † direct thy steps to eternal life; and keep thy foot from being moved.

After this, the Priest blesses the neophyte saying:

PRIEST. — Peace be with thee, saved through God.

THE CATECH. OR GODFATHER. — And with thy spirit.

Now they sing a Hymn:

HYMN.

God has spoken from on high, hear ye people of the earth; hear Him who came and saved all creatures. Let us invoke His name, and send praises to Him on high.

We were called a new Israel in Christ; we became heirs of the Lord and coheirs with Christ,

1 Psalm. LIst. 10
2. Ephesians VI. 16.

then we should invoke the name of the Lord, and send praise to Him on high.

We have tasted the stone of life, and know that the Lord is gracious ; and through faith we were anointed with the oil of holiness, then let us invoke the name of Lord, and give praise to Him on high.

To thee we confide, who art mother and maid-servant of Christ: we should invoke the name of the Lord, and respectfully honour thee.

Now the Priest taking the clothes in his hand, says the following prayer:

PRIEST. — Thou art blessed, Lord omnipotent, Father and sender of our Lord Jesus Christ; who didst deliver this Thy servant from the gloomy dominion of the enemy, and didst call him through this holy fountain, to the light of truth. Bless † Lord now this crown and the clothes, which are a mark of light; that he may entirely take root and grow greatly through Thy immoveable hope, that he may walk in the light of Thy countenance, and rejoice always before Thy face, and glorify the Father, the Son, and the Holy Ghost; now etc.

Ending this prayer he gives orders to clothe the newly baptized child; and puts on his head the crown which was prepared in the beginning of the ceremony of baptism with a small cross fastened at the end of it; when clothed, he covers him with a white coat, and gives into his hands two wax candles, red and green; after which he recites the following prayer:

PRIEST. — Thou art blessed, careful God, who hast clothed Thy servant with a garment of salvation and with a coat of joy; and hast put on his head a helmet of redemption and a crown of graces, as a perfect armor against the adversary. For which thing we too shall glorify gratefully, the Father, the Son, and the Holy Ghost; now and throughout all ages.

Peace † be to all. Let us adore God.

Lord God who lovest men and art merciful, we pray and supplicate Thee; as Thou didst make worthy this Thy servant for Thy blessed hope and Thy eternal redemption, through the regeneration of the water and spirit, grant to him the gifts of peace and of Thy Holy Spirit that come from this consecration, and to attain to Thy eternal and true light; number him among the company of saints that are in heaven, and make him worthy of Thy glorious kingdom; preserve in peace his coming in and his going out, through our Lord Jesus Christ. With whom, together with the Father and the Holy Ghost belong glory, power, and honour; now and troughout all ages.

After this prayer is ended,' the Priest takes the newly baptized-if he be a child in his arms - and brings him up the steps of the altar, and makes him adore before the holy altar and before the holy Cross, kissing the altar on the three sides, as well as the Cross, saying:

PRIEST. — (N. N.) servant of Jesus Christ, coming by his own will from the state of a catechumen to that of baptism, and from baptism to the adoration, worships before this holy altar; he, who cast off from his person his iniquity, and has clothed himself with the light of the knowledge of God; in the name of the Father, of the Son, and of the Holy Ghost. Amen.

Afterwards he gives the Neophyte into the arms of the Godfather, and recites this prayer:

PRIEST. — Lord God omnipotent, Father of our Lord Jesus Christ; to Thee the faithful bow down their heads. Extend Thy invisible hand, and bless them, and favour the works of their hands; fortify those who are in the state of virginity; and strengthen with chastity all men to walk piously in the love of God. Preserve in peace this child, nourish him and make him grow old in years. Protect all men under their own roof, granting them every kind of joy in our Lord Jesus Christ; with whom to Thee Father and to Thy Holy Ghost belong glory, power and honour, now and throughout all ages.

This prayer ended, if the newly baptized be an adult, he administers to him the holy Sacrament of communion, saying:

PRIEST. — May the body of our Lord Jesus Christ save thee and lead thee to eternal life; amen.

After all this accompanying him to the door of the church, he recites the XXXIId psalm; at the end of which, he adds: *Glory be to the Father*, etc.

At the door of the church the Deacon preaches:

DEACON. — Let us again pray the Lord for peace.

For the assistance and salvation that come from heaven, and for the perseverance of this our neophyte, let us pray the Lord, and unitedly say.

The Priest says three times:

Lord have mercy upon us.

PRIEST. — Glory be to Thee eternal king, who didst increase and fill Thy Church with the light of the faith of that multitude, that were saved through the true knowledge of God, preached by Thy Christ; - whom by a spiritual regeneration Thou hast made worthy to be affiliated to Thee, Celestial Father, by making them participate worthily in the body and in the blood of Thy only son. And now, Lord, keep him in the sanctity of Thy Holy Spirit; that he may be irreproachable in doing Thy will, and with innocence reach to eternal life. And all of us allied to him, bless by the grace and mercy of our Lord Jesus Christ, to whom belong glory, power, and honor: now and throughout all ages. Amen.

Peace † be to all. Let us adore God.

Peace, and Creator of peace, Jesus Christ, eternal Priest, and anointed of the Father; behold Thy servant (N. N.) has received Thy holy ointment. We pray Thee Lord, let his name not be blotted out from the book of life; and let us also be worthy of Thy glory, when Thou wilt crown Thy saints, and those who have loved Thy name; and we will incessantly glorify the Father, the son, and the Holy Ghost; now and throughout all ages.

HYMN

O Thou, Holy Trinity, who art glorified by the glory of Thy greatness: make worthy of the glory of Thy celestial inheritance, us, who were born by the holy fountain.

Thou, Lord, who rejoicesth in the blood of martyrs; through their intercession, make worthy of the glory of Thy celestial inheritance, us, who were born by the holy fountain.

We praise Thee in Thy holiness; through the intercession of the Holy Mother of God, make worthy of the glory of Thy celestial inheritance, us, who were born by the holy fountain.

DEACON. — By the Holy Cross let us pray God, that by it He may deliver us from sin, and save us by His merciful grace. O Lord our God all powerful, save us and have mercy upon us.

PRIEST. — Protector and Hope of the faithful, Christ our God, keep Thy servant in peace, in the shadow of Thy Holy and venerable Cross. Deliver him from the enemy, visible and invisible; make him worthy to praise and to glorify Thee with the Father, and the Holy Spirit, now and throughout all ages. Amen.

Blessed be our Lord Jesus Christ. Our Father, who art in heaven, etc.

Prayer for taking away the crown from the head of the baptized ones.

On the eighth day after the baptism, the Priest takes the crown from the head of the new baptized, and recites the following prayer upon him:

Priest. — Thou Lord who didst purify those who were baptized and enlightened; grant them to remain firm in Thy purification. Keep them, Lord, immoveable, in thy graces, that Thou hast given them; remove them from the seduction of the enemy, from his deceptions, and from the deeds of iniquity; that by the light of Thy wisdom he may keep Thy precepts, and with irreproachable conduct, he may attain the peace Thou hast promised. Send Thy Angel of peace to keep him. And may we all be worthy through hope, for the coming of our Lord Jesus Christ. With whom, to Thee Father as well as to Thee, Holy Ghost, belong glory, power, and honour, now and throughout all ages.

Blessed be our Lord Jesus Christ. Our Father, etc.

Rules for the ceremony which is to be performed upon the child after his fortieth day.

In the fortieth day of the existance of the child, the nurse brings the Catechumen to the door of the Church, accompanied by the Mother. The Priest, together with the Deacon, recites the LIst. psalm. After which they chant the following hymn:

HYMN.

Thou, Word, who art before all eternity, and hast taken human nature from the Virgin; to-day Thou didst come into the temple to fulfil the laws, for the salvation of gentiles.

Thou who sittest upon an immaterial throne, and art praised by the Angels; to-day wast raised in the arms of Simeon, that Thou mightest offer to us Thy eternal life.

Thou who art the deliverer of the captives and granter of gifts to all; to-day, through the intercession of the old man, deliver me also, who am a great sinner, from the bonds of death, and make me worthy of Thy eternal life.

At the end of the hymn, the Priest recites the following prayer for the Mother of the Child.

PRIEST. — Lord our God, who didst come to save men; look upon this Thy maid-servant, and grant her to confide in Thy holy catholic and apostolic Church, and to participate in Thy precious and holy body and blood. Wash from her body the impurity, and from her soul the stain, now that are accomplished the forty days; and purify her through the grace of the prayers, of the precious ministry of the pristhood. And make her worthy to enter into the temple of Thy holy glory; and to enjoy the infinite benefits that are promised by Thee. And to Thee belong glory, power and honour, now and throughout all ages.

And for the Child he recites this prayer.

PEACE ✝ be to all. Let us adore God.

Lord God, who renewest those that are grown old and givest life to the human race; Thou art our strength and our resource, who confide in Thee. May the grace of Thy mercy be immoveable from this catechumen, who, of forty days, comes and stays here, that through the protection of Thy holy arm, he may be strong and fearless of the influence of the enemy; as Thou Lord art near all men, and beneficent to all. Keep him, and sanctify through Thy truth; and make him worthy, to receive with sanctity the pledge of Thy Holy Spirit, to enter into Thy holy temple. We pray Thee, Lord, that Thy Holy

Spirit may come upon him, the Spirit of Truth, the Spirit of mildness, and the Spirit of affiliation; that he may be without stain and pure, and may be crowned, with Thy Cross in Thy right hand, and be made coheir with Thy beloved saints in the kingdom of heaven by Thee, our Lord Jesus Christ. To whom belong glory, power, and honour, now and throughout all ages.

At the end of this prayer the Priest orders them to enter into the church, and he recites the XLIIId psalm; at the end of which he says;

Glory be to the Father, etc.

DEACON. — In the name of this holy Church let us pray God, that he may deliver us from sin, and save us by His merciful grace. All-powerful Lord, our God, save us and have mercy on us.

The Priest says three times:

Lord have mercy upon us.

PRIEST. — Within the precincts of this temple, and in the presence of these sacred and divine emblems, bowing in the holy place, we adore with trembling, and we glorify Thy holy, admirable, and victorious dominion, and we offer to Thee benediction and glory, together with the Father and the Holy Spirit now and throughout endless ages.

Then they bend the knee before the holy altar, and the Priest recites this prayer upon the child of forty days and his mother.

PRIEST. — Lord our God, who after forty days, according to the laws, wast presented in the temple, together with Mary, Thy Mother, and wast carassed in the arms of Simeon the just. We pray Thee, Lord; accept this child (N. N.) Thy servant; keep and make him grow through the grace of Thy invisible power; and make him worthy to arrive to share the inheritance of Thine elected, and participate in Thy precious body and blood; and be preserved through the grace of the consubstantial and indivisible Holy Trinity. And to Thee, together with the Father and the Holy Ghost, belong Glory, power, and honour; now, etc.

Now the Priest takes the Child in his arms and brings him up before the altar, where he makes him adore God, saying:

PRIEST. — (N. N.) newly consecrated catechumen, servant to Jesus Christ, of forty days coming into this temple to adore before this holy altar, bows down in the name of the Father, of the Son, and of the Holy Ghost. Amen.

Then he places the child upon the step of the altar, on the right side, and puts his right hand upon his head, and chants the following hymn:

HYMN.

Mother of God, door of heaven; with a divine voice the angel declared: Hail, full of grace, the Lord is with thee.

He who sitteth upon the Cherubim with the Father, was pleased to dwell in thy womb incorruptible; hail, full of grace, the Lord is with thee.

He who was surrounded and watched by the flaming seraphim; to-day was seen among men and in the arms of a terrestrial one; hail, full of grace, the Lord is with thee.

Then he orders the Nurse, to take the child and to give him into the arms of his mother:

DEACON. — By the holy Cross, let us pray God, that by it He may deliver us from sin, and save us by His merciful grace. O Lord our God all-powerful, save us and have mercy upon us.

The Priest says three times:

Lord have mercy upon us.

The Priest then putting his right hand upon the head of the Child and of the Mother, says:

PRIEST. — Guardian and Hope of the faithful, Christ our God, keep Thy servants in peace, under the shadow of Thy Holy and venerable Cross; deliver us from the enemy, visible and invisible; make us worthy to thank and to glorify Thee with the Father and the Holy Spirit, now, etc.

Blessed be our Lord Jesus Christ. Our Father, who art in heaven, etc.